AUG   2009

Practical Ideas
for Small Spaces

Practical Ideas
for Small Spaces

LOFT

Editorial coordination:
Cristina Paredes Benítez

Texts:
Aitana Lleonart Triquell

Art director:
Mireia Casanovas Soley

Cover and layout design:
Claudia Martínez Alonso

English translation: Lynda Trevitt/Equipo de Edición
Copyediting and layout: Equipo de Edición
Equipo de Edición
Dr. Nubiola i Espinós 6-8, Of. 8
08028 Barcelona, Spain
P: +34 934 903 283

Editorial project:
2008 © LOFT Publications
Via Laietana 32, 4º Of. 92
08003 Barcelona, Spain
P: +34 932 688 088
F: +34 932 687 073
loft@loftpublications.com
www.loftpublications.com

ISBN: 978-84-96936-30-0

Printed in China

INDEX

INTRODUCTION

The concept of the home has changed continually throughout history. The most basic constructions at first had just the one space in which all the functions were unified. In colder areas, there was a fire in the middle of the room and the other elements spread around it. This meant the whole space could be heated while the fire was being used for cooking.

As time went on, man began to distinguish day or common zones from night ones. Bedrooms were separated from the rest of the home, which slowly began to integrate different spaces for each use. Today, in a very distinct and evolved fashion, it appears we are returning to some of the features of ancient homes, as once again we are joining rooms together and reducing areas—not for purely aesthetic reasons, however, but mainly because of a lack of space.

Various factors have contributed to the proliferation of small homes. One is the high price of land. More and more people are choosing to live in cities, where small dwellings are usually found, and so there has been a growth in demand unmatched by a rise in supply, leading to increased land prices. Another reason is the change in family types. Throughout history it has been considered normal for various generations of the same family to share the family home all their lives. Today family models have changed. Nuclear families are usually reduced to just two genera-

tions, i.e., parents and children, and often homes are occupied only by couples or even sole individuals.

The reduction in the home's surface area has led to a need to develop ways to integrate all of a space's necessary functions in a practical and cozy fashion. Design aspects can be considered when a home is still being planned, prior to the building and distribution of the rooms. This makes it possible to fit it out to make the most of each of its features and apply optimal spatial solutions that match the need of the person who will inhabit it. One common practice consists of taking advantage of the double height of some properties. High ceilings make it possible to install an upper level or platform where you can put a bedroom, study or other rooms, leaving a great deal more floor area free on the floor below, which can then be used for the rest of the functions. Partitions in this type of apartment are extremely delicate, because the more separations there are, the more the feeling of space will be reduced. This is when you have to decide which rooms you should separate and which are best to unify in a single space. There are other solutions, such as container modules, i.e., small structures that enclose the kitchen or bathroom and which are normally positioned in the center of the home.

Furniture is vital when it comes to small dwellings. Many manufacturers have now added a large number of items to their furniture collections that address space problems or

combine various functions. However, the most common practice, and even the most recommendable in some cases, is to choose custom-made furniture. This means it can be adapted to the unique characteristics of each space and the particular requirements of each occupant. You can find extendable pieces semi-concealed in a single structure, e.g., a dining table which includes cupboards and multiple storage spaces.

The décor, which also includes the wall color as well as the flooring and ceiling, is another basic element that should be carefully considered in small spaces. Of course, pale tones are best for paintwork, furniture and textile elements. The fewer bright colors and patterns used, the bigger the room will seem. The choice of color range is closely linked to the lighting, particularly during the daytime. It is important to consider the number of entries of light and the size of the openings in each room to be decorated. If there is not much natural light, it will be necessary to choose pale colors for the walls and furniture in order to make the most of their special ability to reflect the light. Decorative elements are just as important, as they can be used to create a personal feel that responds to your own particular aesthetic taste. Just remember that instead of many small pieces, you should choose fewer complements with a more impressive and unique character to mark your style without swamping the space.

In small homes there are often certain areas to which little attention is paid. This can include outdoor spaces such as balconies, terraces, courtyards and even rooftops. These areas, even if not protected, can be converted into complementary and popular spaces, particularly during the warmer parts of the year. You can design different spaces, from an outdoor living area to a relaxation zone, simply by the way you arrange the outdoor furniture and by using decorative elements like plants and flowers.

What you must remember is that, even though a home is small, there are many solutions and tricks to maximize its possibilities and achieve a modern, welcoming look.

This is one of the most important and essential points in the design of any space. It is necessary to be aware of a property's size and potential, although you do not have to achieve a single, particular space for each function as it is often necessary for one area or even one piece of furniture to perform various functions. Every home has two well-differentiated zones: the day and night areas. The day areas are where you find the common spaces such as the kitchen, living and dining rooms, while the night area is formed by the bedrooms. The first step is to decide whether you want to separate the two areas or have them coexist in a single space, i.e., make the home into a loft-style dwelling. There are other ways of subtly dividing the two areas, e.g., walls that do not go all the way up to the ceiling; modules used as separators, or bedrooms raised on a structure by way of a platform. This makes it possible to differentiate rooms in line with their functions without having to put up walls or partitions.

In the majority of cases there is one solution that can make the most of the available space: it involves earmarking the home's principal space, normally the biggest, to the kitchen, din-ing and living areas to make a large open-plan space that also ensures the different functions are close to hand. To reinforce the personality of each zone and separate them visually, you can either use different materials in each, create height differences in the floor or ceiling or simply choose diverse colors and tones. Lighting plays an important role here, as the positioning of the different points of light in each zone will make it possible to create an individual focus. Furniture can also function as a separator. For example, a kitchen island can delimit one space from another, or a low sideboard can be placed behind the sofa to face the dining room, with the added advantage that it is somewhere to store household items.

Depending on its size and distribution, each house lends itself to one possibility or another and the secret is choosing the best. Sometimes it is necessary to eliminate some rooms or functions in favor of other, more elemental ones. This shouldn't be a problem: solutions abound that let you combine one or two functions in a single small room such as a bedroom or study. In bathrooms, towel racks, shelves and washbasins suspended from the wall are very useful.

A simple white module subtly divides the living and dining rooms with no need to raise a partition.

MULTIPLE USES OF A SINGLE SPACE

Sometimes you don't have to eliminate functions or areas just because space is tight in the zone where they should be located. You can get a single space to play various functions by using convertible furniture or other recourses. For example, a bedroom can include a small study. Some tables can fold up against the wall and be pulled out by extending the support arm. In other words, the top can hang vertically against the wall and not take up space when not being used. Various pieces of factory-built furniture (which can also be made-to-measure) include a bed and study space in a single module of two different heights: the bed is positioned on top of a space for a desk or where you can put a wardrobe or chest of drawers.

Some eat-in kitchens include bars that can act as a dining table with the addition of stools, or islands where the tops can be extended at one end to sit down for a meal. This means they function like a breakfast bar but can be hidden away when not required. If the living room can't fit a table, you can use a coffee table equipped with a system that raises it to sofa height to make an improvised dining table.

Putting the television in a small space at the foot of the bed lets you watch the screen from the living room and the space the bedroom occupies.

The possibility of using wireless computers and PC peripherals makes it possible to set up a study in any corner of the home.

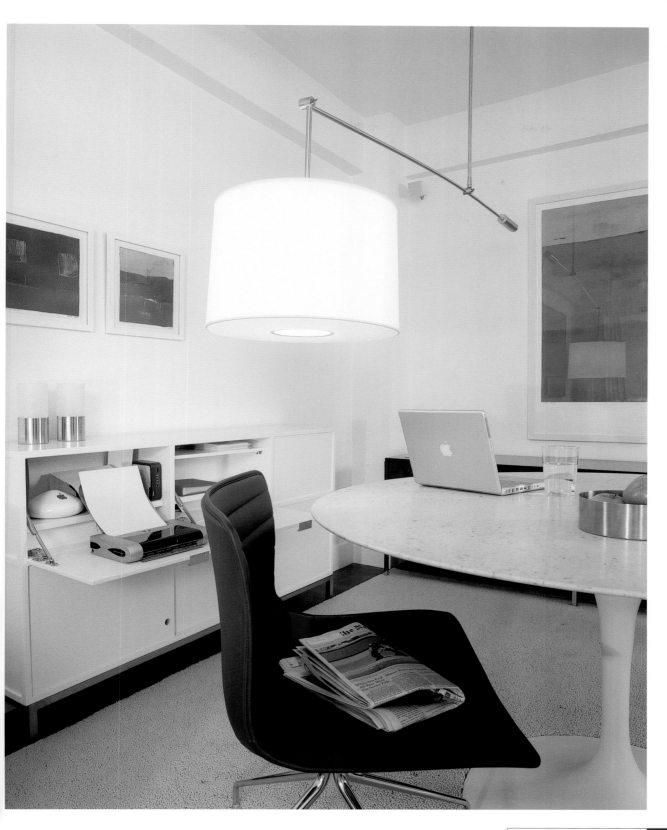

The furniture can be organized so the same area has three different purposes: library, study and dressing room.

A folding bed has been installed in part of the living room of this home. This solution can be applied in the main bedrooms or guest rooms.

UNIFIED SPACES

To avoid separation elements, which markedly reduce the feeling of space, a good idea is to design different functions that can share a space. You can use the perimeter of the property to mark each use, e.g., the kitchen, dining and living areas. Each will form a defined zone against one wall or in one corner of the space. Another solution is to put the kitchen opposite the living room with a dining table in the middle to create a separation by way of the furniture.

If you want to emphasize or in some way delimit each function without concrete divisions, you can do so visually by using elements such as the flooring, walls or ceiling. You can subtly mark out each zone by changing the material the floor is covered in, or simply by changing its color or texture. Wall paint is another practical alternative, as changing the color or tone can create a visual separation. A third option consists of changing the floor height. You can achieve separate spaces by raising some areas, using timber flooring, or even by lowering the ceiling.

The picture on the right shows how changing the color of the wall and kitchen furniture creates a gradual aesthetic transition between the kitchen and the living room.

A large open space makes it possible to situate different areas—kitchen, dining room, living room and bedroom—in a more rational fashion.

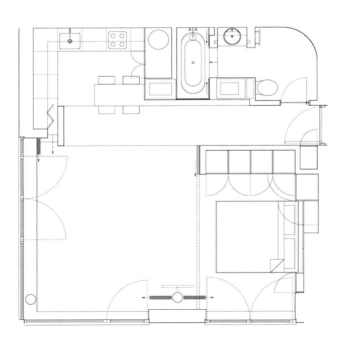

Plan

- Unify spaces: it will prevent the need for partitions which considerably reduce space and mobility.

- Choose an eat-in kitchen that opens onto the dining room or living room. This will prevent divisions and gain mobility in the space.

- Design spaces on different levels if the ceiling height permits. A second floor can be used for a bedroom, for example, to gain useable space.

- Create too many divisions so each function is met in a different space unrelated to the rest.

- Use big staircases to join two levels together. Some styles let you keep the bottom space free—perfect for positioning a bookshelf.

- Visually separate the two levels in homes with a second floor. For safety, add a railing or low wall.

The kitchen and dining room of this home can be separated, but joining them together creates the perception of more space.

The kitchen, dining and living rooms are in a single space without divisions, facilitating communication between them.

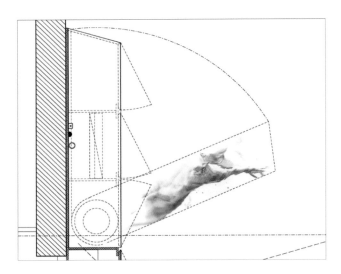

Details of table movement.

A sliding table hidden in a mirror-covered module doubles the use of this space and creates a dining room where the living room was.

DOUBLE HEIGHTS AND SPLIT LEVELS

In some small properties, features of the ceiling or roof make it possible to maximize space. Homes built in disused factory buildings or from the division of older, larger houses often feature high ceilings where you can install an upper level for some rooms, usually the bedroom or study, and reserve the lower floor for the day areas. To reach the upper level you just need a simple stepladder, or stairs as small as possible to safeguard the usable space. These upstairs rooms can open onto the rest of the property through the use of a railing or medium height wall. This recourse also enables the natural light to illuminate both floors.

Another possibility is to find an apartment with a vaulted ceiling, something not uncommon in penthouses. The low area where the sloping ceiling and walls meet consumes a lot of space and hinders distribution, although there are ways to get around it: the bedroom can be put here, with the bed positioned under the slope so that the headboard is at the highest end. Another idea is to use the low area to install a small television module.

This apartment has been designed around a central zone. The partial-height partitions make it look more spacious.

The plans show the mezzanine level that has been built by taking advantage of the double height of the apartment. A simple spiral staircase provides access to the bedroom.

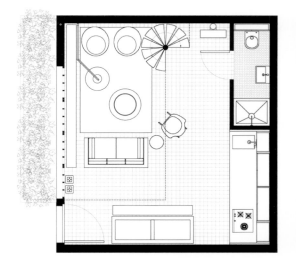

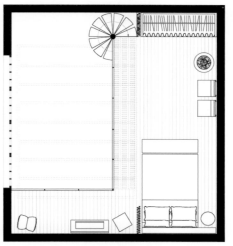

Plans

Double height makes it possible to magnify the area of a home. Here a second bedroom has been installed on the top floor.

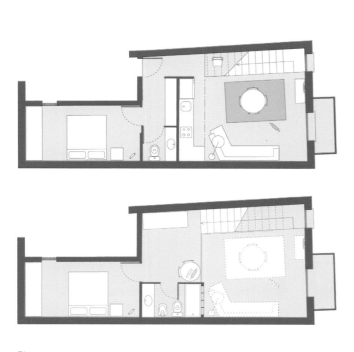

Plan

The high ceilings in this small New York apartment have been used to make a floor with a study.

PARTITIONS

When a space is small, the use of partitions becomes very delicate. Of primary importance is each owner's particular preference, i.e., the space they want to isolate from the rest. The bedroom, kitchen and bathroom are the areas usually given their own space for maximum convenience. Bear in mind that as well as wall partitions, there are many other solutions which can also have added advantages such as flexibility of space. Low partition or unfinished walls that save having to have doors and shelter different areas are one solution. There are other options, too, such as sliding or folding panels made from different materials which can be moved in line with your requirements. If you choose translucent materials like glass or plexiglass sheets you can noise-proof and even smell-proof a space, but you won't be isolating it visually, which means you still have the feeling of space. Curtains and folding screens are other elements that can help divide a room. It is even common and practical to use pieces of furniture to separate two rooms.

Right: Glass separates the entrance from the rest of the apartment—practical solution when you want to divide small spaces.

The renovation of the apartment has modified the room distribution. Sliding translucent-glass panels separate the kitchen from the bedroom.

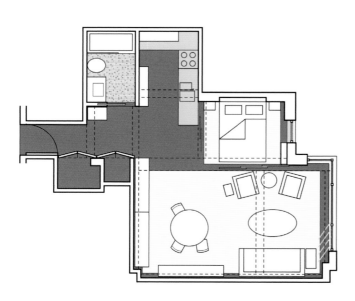

Plan

The timber panels slide across to close off the bedroom. The dark timber unifies the look of the apartment.

A large sliding panel separates the living room from the bedroom, a small, minimalist space that includes a bed, wardrobe and television.

Plan

Panels which separate rooms and can be custom-made to the customer's taste are a functional and decorative item at the same time.

Tips 10

1 To make a space feel bigger, avoid using separations as much as possible, especially ones that consist of walls and partitions.

2 If ceiling height permits, you can design a top floor for rooms such as a bedroom or study.

3 In properties with a diaphanous space, you can unify some zones instead of designing divisions.

4 The use of sliding doors frees up passages because you don't have to keep the area occupied by regular doors clear.

5 Instead of enclosing the kitchen in a different room, you could choose an eat-in style which optimizes space and leaves it free.

6 Swapping the bathtub for a shower tray gives this room increased mobility.

7 In some cases you can have the bedroom and study in the same space, e.g., by raising the bed and positioning a desk beneath it.

8 To make the most of a zone with a sloping ceiling, put the bed beneath it or add low closets.

9 In duplexes it is best not to completely close off the top floor but allow it to look down onto the floor below.

10 Very often irregularities in a home's perimeter can be used to put each area in a specific space, adapting it to the shape.

FURNITURE AND STORAGE

The choice of furniture is essential to the decoration of small homes. Furniture should offer everything you need to go about your daily activities and at the same time provide spaces for storing household items and personal objects. It is a good idea to choose practical pieces in clean lines, as their straight angles can be easily adapted to position other items in a row. You should also bear in mind the wide range of convertible and folding furniture which will free up space when packed away. After choosing the basic pieces like the bed, sofa, table and wardrobe, think about all the complementary items that also have necessary functions. Living-room closets, sideboards and bookshelves include storage space and are a way of keeping your belongings in order, something of utmost importance when space is at a premium. Apart from the big-ticket items, which as well as cupboards and drawers include television modules and the like, there are more original solutions. If you choose one of these, it is best to go for clean lines and pale colors, particularly white, as large items of furniture will subtract a lot of visual space from the home.

If the bedroom does not have built-in closets but there is a wall big enough for a large wardrobe, it will be better in the long run to have one custom-made to fill the whole length of the wall from floor to ceiling. This will ensure you can use the space to the full. If you don't like sofa beds, you can choose a storage bed with an empty space in the middle, or raise the bed on a structure with closets or bookshelves, for example. This is a common choice in children's and teenagers' rooms, where you can also use bunk beds.

Other items such as trunks, stackable boxes and small containers are great to use with wardrobes as they let you organize and store clothes and other objects in any spare bit of space.

The kitchen is another area where furniture and storage solutions are crucial. For galley-style kitchens, it is important to use every corner to put a cupboard or drawers, both below the bench top and above it, and it is a good idea to never use dark colors for these items.

Hallways and corridors are perfect for small items of furniture or bookshelves, if size permits. In the entrance, a small chest of drawers or sideboard will allow you to store keys and umbrellas.

A bright module that turns on an axis can change the position of the TV and separate the two rooms.

CONVERTIBLE AND
MADE-TO-MEASURE FURNITURE

This is best when it comes to decorating small rooms. Convertible furniture provides creative and very practical solutions to problems of space and can cover various functions in one piece. The key element is the table. There are various types, including extension and folding tables. Extension tables take up very little room but can accommodate more diners, as the top can be pulled out using a simple mechanism. Folding tables take up even less space, as they are made of a support with flaps that can be raised at either end to form the usable surface. Some pieces of living-room furniture contain these types of tables inside them or have one space from which the table top protrudes and another for storing folding chairs.

Then there is made-to-measure furniture: the big advantage here is that it can adapt to the particular features of each home. Custom-made furniture aims to maximize space and make the most of every last inch of usable surface. These pieces can be commissioned separately, on a piece-by-piece basis, or all at once, designing complete structures that run from one wall to another and which have various functions and additional recourses, such as blocks for seats with an empty space for storage, one of the most notorious problems with small homes.

This module can slide across to open up the space to other rooms in the home, while also creating an interesting interplay of volumes and colors.

Made-to-measure furniture, such as in this kitchen, can be adapted to the customer's requirements with regards measurements and colors and even fixtures and fittings.

This module, custom-made by the architects, contains the kitchen plus storage space. The design and color unify the look of the apartment.

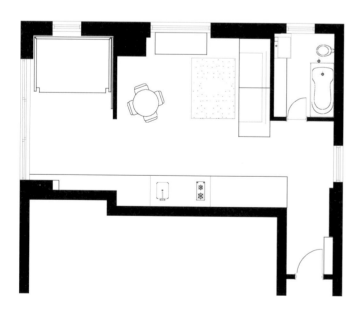

Plan

Instead of raising a partition to separate the rooms, a module that can turn 90° achieves the same result. It also drastically changes the look of the inside of the apartment.

INTERIOR MODULES

To avoid renovation work and having to build walls or partitions, there is a solution that makes it possible to separate one or various rooms in an original fashion. It involves using interior modules, i.e., structures (normally square or rectangular) that contain the kitchen or bathroom (usually, although they can contain other rooms). They permit some functions to be separated from others in a different and daring manner, as they usually come in bright colors.

These types of modules are mostly found in loft-style apartments, as they enable the remaining space to be distributed on either side of the module. Private zones like the bedroom can be positioned behind the module. This achieves a certain degree of privacy, as the inside of the module is partially hidden from view from the other zones of the property.

The bathroom and kitchen com[...] together in this module designe[...] by i29, specialists in this type [...] construction.

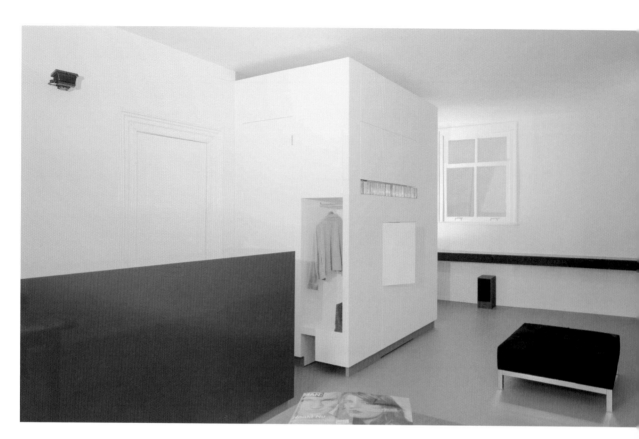

Some of the materials used in the modules are synthetic resins, which are very resistant and durable.

This module designed by Studioata conceals a bathroom with a shower. The volume is like a sculpture that decorates and separates the kitchen from the living room.

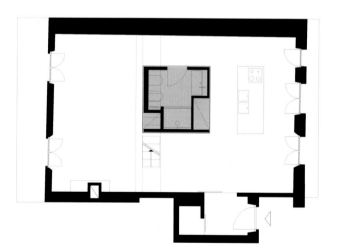

Plan

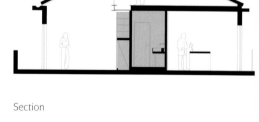

Section

KITCHENS AND BATHROOMS

These have a number of added difficulties as they require certain indispensable elements that take up a fair amount of space. It is necessary to find a way to combine the basic pieces with the other materials needed and to have empty spaces for storing household items (in the case of the kitchen) or personal objects (in the case of the bathroom). Electrical household appliances and bathroom goods usually come in standard sizes, although some manufacturers have now started producing them in different dimensions to offer solutions to the new needs and demands.

Mobility is another major challenge in these two areas. In the case of kitchens, the distribution permits more freedom as there are various ways of laying out the space and its parts: galley-style, with an island, u-shaped, open-plan or inserted in a module, etc. The bathroom is more complicated because here the parts are usually positioned in a particular fashion and changing them can be tricky. You will have to find solutions for storage and the disposition of other items, without putting too many elements on the ground as this can hamper mobility.

Bathrooms in small flats are not usually very big; a vanity cabinet with drawers right down to the floor provides more space.

Shelves above the toilet create space for personal items and make the most of an under-used area.

Kitchens

There are many kitchen combinations that adapt to each type of space. Galley-style kitchens enable you to put all the electrical household appliances in a row and can open out onto other zones of the home. In some cases you can use sliding doors or panels to close off the kitchen when you want to hide it from the other rooms. One type of very practical kitchen often found in small dwellings is the eat-in kitchen, normally shaped in an L or a U and featuring a breakfast bar which also acts as a separation element. Cabinets and drawers can be positioned underneath the bar and others set in the wall. This keeps the rest of the kitchen free for the electrical household appliances and other cupboards. Another option is kitchen furniture which, once all the appliances have been gathered up, completely conceals the work areas. This generally involves custom-made furniture with sliding doors or panels used to hide each element. Although islands take up a lot of space, they can be great if you choose a model with sliding bench tops which, once pulled out, expose the work zone, while the movable piece becomes a dining table.

The decorated kitchen-cabinet doors break with the monochromatic uniformity of many of these rooms.

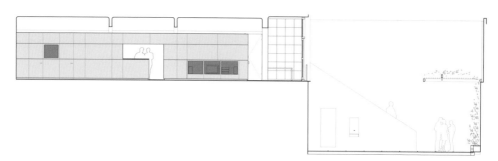

Section

Plan

The kitchen island facilitates circulation. The distribution of the
cabinets has made it possible to
install a table in the middle.

Plan

Bathrooms

The bathroom has certain basic requirements met by parts such as the shower or tub, the toilet, washbasin and bidet. These items are often essential and require a particular location, affecting the space available for the other parts. One practical solution is to position a washbasin in a piece of furniture with cupboards and drawers, or in a structure which includes a mirror with lights at the top to improve and complement the lighting. Hanging cabinets are great too, as they do not obstruct mobility within the bathroom. Some include a mirror at the front and can be placed on top of the washbasin, thus joining two functions in a single piece. If you can choose the basic elements, it is better to install a shower tray rather than a standard bathtub, which gobbles up twice the space. The remaining area can be used for tall, narrow cabinets for storing towels and toiletry products. Shelves are another very practical recourse in this part of the home, particularly ones made from glass. They can be positioned between the mirror and washbasin to provide handy access to toiletry products. Corner soap racks can be installed inside the shower and the rest of the space left free. Heated towel racks serve a double purpose, as well as add comfort.

Taking advantage of the double height of this home made it possible to put the bathroom underneath the bed and increase the functionality of this zone.

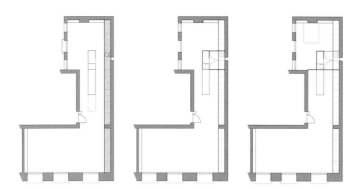

Plan. Enclosed bathroom.

A number of panels enclose the bathroom, which uses the circulation space between the shower, next to the kitchen, and the closet that conceals the toilet.

LIVING ROOMS, STUDIES AND BEDROOMS

These are probably the rooms that allow the most creativity and flexibility in the whole of the home. There are numerous ideas in terms of furniture and complements that combine practicality and good looks. The three areas have very clear functions within a home's requirements. Bedrooms and living rooms should offer a space to relax and wind down in, with furniture that combines comfort with storage and organizational solutions. In studies it is necessary to have a fairly large desk, as well as shelves, drawers and bookcases for keeping items.

These spaces have a big advantage in that they are not constrained by a need to include parts that require a specific loca-tion because of connections to pipes or other conduits. Their distribution only has to respond to practical and aesthetic fac-tors. The depth of furniture is a very important aspect. Many pieces, such as bookshelves and sideboards, are 15 to 19 inches deep, although you can also find a great variety with a depth of 11 inches and which are the most suitable for small spaces. It is a good idea to use low or medium-height furniture in the living room, bedroom and study, except for wardrobes, which should be as large as possible. This will enhance the feeling of space and mobility, as the walls are on show and demonstrate the real reference perimeter.

A transparent table and two poufs, less bulky than sofas, visu-ally lighten this space.

Living Rooms

The living room is one of the busiest areas in any home. It is the space devoted to relaxation, where you can wind down from your daily activity. It is also the area for social and family get-togethers and should include parts that make it a welcoming zone. The main item is the sofa, which must be comfortable and which can be problematic if there is not a lot of space. Simple two or three-seat sofas can be complemented with poufs as leg rests, and some even include a footrest operated by a lever. If the area reserved for the sofa is in a corner, there are a number of models that can adapt to this shape.

As with some beds, there are sofas with an empty space for storing things inside them. Living-room furniture is essential. These days, low television modules with drawers and cabinets are becoming increasingly popular. A low height makes the room feel bigger. It is a good idea to choose medium-height furniture for complementary items such as shelves. In extreme cases where there is no possibility of having a dining table, some coffee tables can be raised to sofa height for eating or to work at with a computer. Some models also have a space for storing magazines or other objects, revealed when the top is lifted.

The use of a low module for the TV and lack of high shelves make this room look spacious and comfortable.

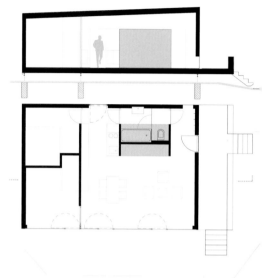

Section and plan.

The glass wall communicates the living room with the outdoors area, increasing the space. Two easy chairs replace the sofa and take up less space.

A nest of tables is a good solution for a small living room. Mirrors visually increase the space and are useful, too.

Studies

Studies are becoming increasingly important in today's homes and often have very particular requirements. With the rise of the computer, the Internet and the increasing trend of working from home, it is practically necessary to have a space exclusively for this function. If that is not possible, studies can also be inserted in an area that can combine two functions, e.g., the living room or bedroom. The desk is the basic element in this space. It must be big enough to afford a comfortable and optimal work area and may be fixed or folding. If the study is located in the space shared with the living or dining room, one very practical idea is to put a bookshelf on one side. This can be used not just to store items such as books, folders and other objects, but can also separate the areas. Sometimes the study is included in the bedroom. Here it is best to earmark a particular corner for the desk, which should include a drawer.

The pictures on the right show an original folding table that can turn the gallery into a study, making the most of the natural light.

The plan shows the opening in the partition that brings more light into the study, situated in the bedroom. The sliding timber panels close off the space if necessary.

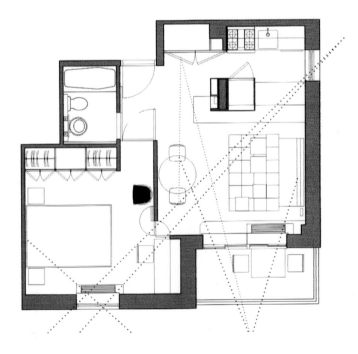

Plan

Bedrooms

One of the main problems with a bedroom is the bed, particularly if it is a double bed, as it is considerably large in size. If you opt for a double bed, there are various solutions, such as folding beds that can be put away inside a wardrobe or large chest. However, for practical purposes it is best to not have to put the bed away and bring it out again each night, and there is a wide range of storage beds that can help. With these, a simple mechanism enables you to lift the mattress from the base with your foot to reveal an empty space the same size as the bed where you can store clothes, shoes and a great many other objects. Or you can have a double-height bed positioned on top of a platform or raised structure and use the space below for other purposes, by putting in wardrobes, drawers or all manner of storage solutions. This option is also very common in children's rooms, where lack of space often makes it necessary to turn to such ideas in order to include a study zone. Bedside tables are another very practical solution, as some include drawers and small cupboards for personal objects. In some corners which at first seem unusable, such as behind the door, you can put a shoe cupboard, shallow enough to not obstruct the passage. Hanging shelves and cupboards are other solutions, although they should be used sparingly to prevent the space from feeling cramped.

A module conceals a folding bed in this small New York apartment. The living room transforms into a bedroom in a matter of seconds.

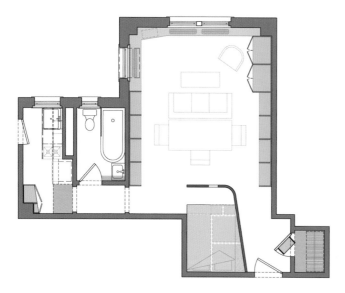

Plan

Renovation work changed the situation of the bedroom, now behind a curved partition wall that does not interrupt communication with the other spaces in the apartment

Tips 10

1 Convertible furniture can reduce the number of pieces needed, as two or more functions can be combined in a single item.

2 To make the most of every square inch you can use custom-made furniture which adjusts to the peculiarities of the home.

3 Folding and extension tables leave free space when not needed and can be easily assembled for use.

4 If you choose to close a space, a good idea is modules, as they avoid the need for walls or partitions.

5 Shelves can be put up anywhere and add an extra support without obstructing the passage.

6 It is a good idea to hang cupboards in the bathroom and they kitchen, as they provide valuable storage solutions.

7 Some coffee tables have an empty space in the middle which can be used to store magazines or other objects.

8 Slightly reducing the depth of furniture will free up space, clear passages and visually increase a room.

9 Low furniture provides a greater feeling of space as it leaves the walls clear so you can appreciate the true perimeter of the property.

10 Storage beds or ones raised on top of a wardrobe or empty space provide more room for storage.

DÉCOR

It is easy to fall into the trap of thinking that décor is an aesthetic element hard to get right in small spaces. This is absolutely not true, as a very personal and unique feel can be created without having to fill the property with a great many objects and complements. The décor begins with the choice of wall color and flooring. For the walls there are many options, ranging from the many styles of paint through to paper and even vinyl, a very fashionable choice in recent seasons. The choice of color will make it possible to create the feeling you want, although there are tricks to making the space look bigger. Painting the ceilings white and even painting just one wall in a chosen color while leaving the rest white visually enlarges any space. The same thing is true with wallpaper. You can choose any pattern or color so long as you do not go overboard with it. Using it on just one side of the room will not only add a feeling of more space but will focus attention on this decorative point. There are many ideas for the floor too, from very-popular polished concrete through to tiles and parquet. You should always try to choose pale tones, regardless of the material used.

Lighting is another determining factor. If the apartment has a good entry or entries of light, it is advisable to not build walls or separations, so the light can reach the maximum profundity of the home. Translucent blinds instead of curtains protect privacy without reducing the intensity of the light because of their minimal opacity.

To complement the natural light in less well-lit areas and during the hours without sunlight, you have to think about the type of light and lamp each room calls for, as the type of activity carried out in each space can influence the choice of clear or yellow tones and bright or soft lighting. As well as the general lighting, the points of light in different corners with specific uses are also important. In order to not detract attention from decorative elements, some pieces of furniture and items have characteristics that merge with the rest of the room, i.e., furniture covered in a way that is similar to the space where it is found or its simplicity detracts attention from it. This makes it possible to play more with decorative elements such as paintings, mirrors, wallpaper, textile items such as curtains and rugs and even complements like plaids and cushions.

A suitable combination of these elements will inject the property with character without swamping any room. The trick is to mix some furniture and complements in clean lines and neutral tones with other more daring pieces that provide personality.

The blue tones that dominate in
this apartment confer elegance
and highlight a minimalist décor.

COLORS

Neutral tones and pale colors are the best choice when it comes to decorating small spaces. The darker the tone, the less the light will reverberate on the surface, reducing the feeling of space. If you want to add a splash of color to a room you should use concentrated, bright tones. Another idea is to add one big note of color while keeping the rest neutral, e.g., by painting just one wall, which will then become the focus of attention. In bedrooms, for example, you could paint the wall near the top of the bed. This makes it the most colorful element in the room and also visually transforms it into a headboard. To increase the depth of different zones it is a good idea to paint the ceiling white, something commonplace in most homes and which is very effective. If you choose to paper the walls, again it is best to use pale tones and delicate patterns. Horizontal stripes can create a certain feeling of space and depth.

To make the most of the available space, furniture should be light-colored, particularly white. For materials such as wood, the lighter the better, e.g., maple or oak. And don't forget substances like glass and plexiglass, which can either be transparent or tinted in different colors. You can play with diverse textures in the textile elements because, as mentioned before, the more neutral the colors, the better - except for cushions and small rugs which can add an invigorating touch of color.

These pictures are a good example of decorating with color. Right: colored sofas against a pale background. Far right: a single wall of color.

The notes of red add freshness and break the monotony of an apartment in which white rules.

The pale walls and floor are the perfect stage for highlighting brighter and more original pieces.

Screen-printed glass with a floral motif and an elegant combination of red and grey form a space with lots of personality.

The white floor and ceilings of this San Sebastian loft merge with the wooden beams to create a cozy interior.

LIGHTING

Lighting is fundamental for the development of daily activity. Plenty of natural light is an asset in any home, as it means not only energy and economic savings but can also be a source of vitality for people. Without a doubt, natural light is much more pleasant than artificial light, which should be reserved for the nighttime hours. Windows and openings are fundamental in any home as they permit the entry of natural light while at the same time prevent a feeling of enclosure. The biggest openings are usually found in the living or living/dining room, where they should be used to maximum advantage. When it comes to hanging curtains, it is best to use flimsy fabrics in pale colors without too big a pattern in order to safeguard privacy without hindering or reducing the entry of light.

You must be very careful with artificial lighting, as you will have to find a particular type of light and lamp to match the function of each room. General lighting, normally involving the use of ceiling or wall lamps, should be pale and abundant, although it is a very good idea to install a regulator to adapt the light intensity and therefore also change a room's mood in order to meet the specific needs of a given moment. General lighting should be complemented with points of light that improve visibility in particular work areas.

In this study, the entry of natural light is toned down by a roller blind that can graduate the effect of the sunlight in line with the needs of each part of the day.

Windows don't only make a room look bigger because they reflect the light; they make it look lighter, too.

The mood lighting and focalized lamps on the dining table create a welcoming look.

Daytime Lighting

To achieve suitable lighting during the day, the first step is to study the layout of the different outdoor openings. If there are not many windows, it is advisable to try to build new ones, as far as possible. This cannot always be done and depends on the type of building and the distribution of the rooms.

Instead of positioning windows from halfway up the wall to the ceiling, it is a good idea to glass in the whole wall, whether there is a terrace or balcony or not. The bottom part can be fixed so that it is only possible to open the sheets of the top frame. There are various types of window openings, other than the typical inward-opening ones, which make it possible to save space. They include sliding windows, which may be simple, with one sheet simply sliding over the other, or more complex, such as folding styles. The latter are a good idea if you have a wide window with a number of frames because, as they are pulled to the sides, they double up on each other next to the wall to achieve the total opening.

Another option consists of the use of pivot windows, which you have to be careful with when using with a curtain because they open inward. If there are various floors, with a mezzanine level or platform for the bed or study, it is best to not completely enclose the upper level but leave some of it open to the lower floor to take advantage of the light that enters from the windows below.

Making the most of the openings in the home, such as in these two pictures, is a good way to increase the amount of natural light that enters the home.

Glass ceilings and skylights are suitable for colder zones with less sunlight, as they reduce these disadvantages even in winter.

A blind is a good way to gain privacy without losing natural light.

NIGHTTIME LIGHTING

Artificial lighting is a reinforcement of the daytime lighting in zones that are less well-lit and also the main source of light during the hours when there is no sunlight. For this reason it is a basic element in which choice, layout and intensity must be specific and suitable for each type of room and function. There are two basic tones of artificial light: clear, white light and warm, yellow-toned light. The former is used for the general lighting of spaces, normally with lamps hanging from the ceiling, wall lamps or ceiling lights. Their clarity achieves complete and general lighting of the area in question and the whiter the light, the greater the feeling of space. This type of lighting can be complemented in particular zones using focalized points of light, which have two basic functions: in some cases they help to reinforce visibility in work zones, such as the dining table, study or kitchen areas, or spaces which require more light, e.g., the entrance hall. In other cases they can create different moods in line with the function of each zone. In the living room, for example, you can install a small lamp with faint yellow light to achieve a warm and relaxing feel. This is good in the bedroom, too. In small spaces it is best to not go overboard with yellow-toned lights, as a warm-looking space can look smaller as well. Instead, go for clear lighting and regulate the intensity according to the need of the moment.

Lamps are functional objects, but groundbreaking modern designs make them very versatile decorative objects, too.

Lighting can be the perfect complement to a more theatrical and daring interior. Here the lamp is a sculpture that decorates with light and shape.

Do

- Use a chromatic color range based on white and pale tones. The softer the colors, the bigger and lighter the space will seem.

- The use of mirrors in areas other than the bathroom and bedroom will give more depth to the space due to the reflection in the mirror.

- Look for decorative elements which have an added use. There are no end of things which complement their use with an original design.

Don't

- Fill the room with different-sized objects. It makes spaces look much smaller and crowded.

- Combine different patterns in the same room. If you want to upholster the sofa and pick curtains, it is best to use the same pattern.

- Use yellow, low-intensity lights for general lighting. The whiter the light, the bigger the space will look.

MATCHING FURNITURE

To prevent against visually obstructing the aesthetic or chromatic harmony in particular spaces, you can use matching furniture and complements. Matching pieces are ones that go practically unnoticed because their characteristics or coverings allow them to blend into the rest of the furniture and decoration. They usually involve large structures, including closets and chests of drawers, and are covered in plain surfaces the same tone as the walls and other elements. Some pieces are completely concealed, as if they were walls, because their handles and knobs have been replaced with other devices and openings that are almost imper-

ceptible. This is a practical idea in homes which, although small, have corridors that are big enough to put a large module that goes right up to the ceiling. It is a good storage solution that you barely even see.

Some kitchens, usually open-plan ones that look onto the dining or living room, have been designed in line with this characteristic. In order to hide the electrical household appliances, sink, kitchen items and different tools from view, some kitchens are designed within a large module which, once closed, conceals them completely. All the elements are protected behind sliding doors and systems.

This solution can be applied with good results anywhere in the home: living room, study, bedrooms, bathrooms or kitchen.

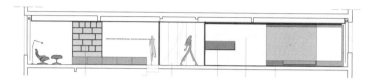

Section

The furniture in this apartment has been designed to barely be seen and achieves a visual continuity throughout the whole of the space.

You can cover electrical household appliances to integrate them with the rest of the furniture and unify the look of the kitchen.

The closets in these photos provide storage space and are camouflaged with the walls of the home thanks to their simple design.

DECORATIVE COMPLEMENTS

The décor of any home begins even when it is empty, without furniture or complements. The wall color and flooring are the first decorative elements to choose and must be complemented with the furniture, both the basic and additional items. Finally you add the complements, i.e., the smaller pieces in each space that help reflect the aesthetic predilections and personality of the owner.

In small dwellings, it is important to not swamp the décor with too many complements. It is better to decide on particular unique pieces that make an impact and which sum up and reflect the desired look. One trick that can give great results is to use a leitmotif throughout the home, or at least in each room. A repeated element can involve the use of the same material in different objects, e.g., a particular tone of timber, or the same color in different objects, e.g., in a magazine rack, coffee table, cushions or wall paintings. The idea is to focus on a single aspect that injects a great deal of personality.

Mirrors hung in different parts of the house can boost the sense of space, as the reflection visually doubles the space and reflects light back into the room. The most common places to use them are the entrance hall and living room, as well as the bathroom and bedrooms. In some cases you can cover walls or the front of a closet in glass to achieve a double function. Textile elements are another decorative device to be considered. They should preferably feature similar patterns or be in pale, neutral tones.

Mirrors or screen-printed glass decorate without increasing the amount or volume of ornamental objects.

Light-colored walls and floors draw attention to the decorative objects, which express the personality of the owners.

Patterns should be used with care and in moderation, but can transform a room into a young, cheerful space.

Tips 10

1 Using white and pale colors on the walls makes a space look much bigger.

2 It is best to avoid dark tones and patterns on walls and furniture.

3 Arranging many small decorative complements can make a room feel crowded. It is better to use a few carefully selected pieces.

4 The bigger the windows and less opaque the curtains, the more light will enter, adding to the feeling of space.

5 When designing the distribution of artificial lighting it is a good idea to choose clear lights for general lighting and reserve warmer tones for mood lights.

6 In homes with unified spaces, you can focus each zone with different lighting to separate them visually.

7 Painting the ceiling white will make any space look deeper.

8 Covering some furniture in plain surfaces with no obvious handles can match them to the walls and make them go practically unnoticed.

9 Mirrors not only reflect the light but reflect the room, too, giving the feeling that it continues beyond its limits.

10 Using small lamps or points of light creates a relaxing, cozy feel in the living room or bedroom.

SMALL OUTDOOR SPACES

Outdoor spaces are often forgotten about, but regardless of whether you have a large courtyard or just a balcony or small terrace, you can convert it into another room of the house. In some properties these spaces are even bigger than the zone earmarked for the indoor dining room and can be used during the warmer months as a place to have lunch or dinner in, or simply as another space. There are many ways to do up outdoor areas and use awnings, large umbrellas, tightened canvases or even gazebos as protection from the sun. There is also a wide range of outdoor furniture in different materials, including tables, chairs, deck chairs and even sofas and small swings to create relaxed environments in which to enjoy the open air. The choice will depend on the space available, as well as the function you want to give this area. To ensure privacy, you can install lattices around the perimeter. Their form protects the space visually without making you feel stressed or claustrophobic, as the gaps allow you see through them. Plants are another solution: not only do they protect your privacy, but they add a fresh touch of nature.

Ground-floor apartments can sometimes include a courtyard out the front, back or in the middle of the building and permit much more freedom in terms of decoration and the way they are fitted out. One very modern trend includes doing up indoor courtyards in a Japanese style, i.e., a zen patio with rounded corners, sand and bamboo, among other materials. In some cases water can be an added element. Here you can also apply the ideas of *feng shui* to achieve a harmonious flow of different energies through the careful arrangement of natural elements.

For floors it is a good idea to use long-lasting, weatherproof materials such as terracotta, although many people go for a plant fiber or mock-effect fitted carpet. Another idea is to create a small garden, but bear in mind they need a lot of work. If space permits, you can even build a small outdoor kitchen, or erect a barbeque or grill, enabling you to cook and eat outdoors and make the most of fine weather.

In terms of decoration, as well as furniture you can play with the disposition of outdoor plants. There are many types, sizes and conditioning factors that will guide your search for species that best adapt to your particular requirements, both in terms of aesthetic preferences and practicality.

TYPES AND USES

Outdoor areas usually come in very different shapes and sizes, from small balconies that cannot even fit a table through to large spaces up to twice as big as the indoor area of the home. When you have very little space it is best not to clutter it with too many objects, plants or complements. Small balconies, common in city apartments, can be spruced up just by hanging window boxes from the railing. As well as the regular forged-iron structures that flowerpots sit in, there are other models, too, e.g., long, rectangular planter boxes which can be positioned as a single piece. An outdoor wall lamp or small hanging lamp with ethnic motifs can set the scene for enjoyable outdoor living. Larger terraces permit greater flexibility and enable you to position a table and chairs. Folding chairs are particularly useful, as you can clear them away if more space is needed.

The biggest advantages in terms of space layout are found in courtyards, which are not only big but can also house storage units such as benches or treated-timber chests with an internal lining to protect them from rain, inside which you can store tools and objects that don't fit within the home.

The white used in this patio, surrounded by other buildings and found in a ground floor apartment, boosts the natural light.

Part of the terrace has been covered to enjoy the space in summer and during the hours when the sun is at its peak.

Patio walls and lattices that separate terraces or gardens are the most suitable places for climbing plants.

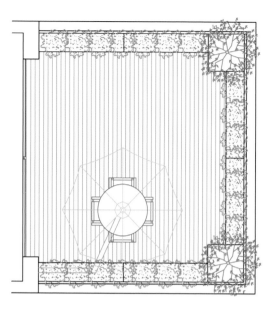

Plan

Window boxes were positioned around the walls of this small patio to make the most of the space.

- Choose furniture made from weatherproof material like treated timber, natural fibers or stainless steel, as they support exposure to the environment.

- In outdoor spaces, use awnings that do not need feet or supports so you don't subtract from the useable space.

- Use folding furniture which can be stacked in a corner or stored inside. If the patio or terrace is small, this will enable it to have different uses.

- Position large plant pots or parterres right around the perimeter of the space as it will subtract from the useable space. It is better to put them in the corners or along just one side.

- Use lattices or other elements to protect privacy that are too high or opaque as they will block the entry of light and create a feeling of enclosure.

- Over-furnish. Determine the main function you want to promote before you start to add the furniture.

MATERIALS AND FURNITURE

It is fundamental for outdoor flooring and furniture materials to be weatherproof. Once this basic premise has been met, there are many designs to choose from. Firstly you should consider the type of flooring you want. Some materials, like plant fibers or artificial grass, can be laid like a carpet to emulate a garden without the trouble the natural product involves or the dedication it requires. Another common choice is outdoor tiles such as terracotta or even treated timber-style tiles which are easy to lift up and clean. Timber flooring is very fashionable right now and looks very elegant. The timber most commonly used is teakwood, although its high cost has led to other, cheaper types of wood being treated for flooring. The most suitable materials for outdoor furniture are teakwood, Chinese oak and cedar. Stainless steel is popular, too. They all stand up well to the sun, rain and humidity, as well as being solid and hard. There are other materials, such as natural fibers like bamboo, rattan and wicker, which do not weather as well but are fresh materials and appropriate for outdoor use. They are recommended for areas under cover, such as a small porch, or beneath an awning or canvas or where they can be protected by balconies on the floors above.

The warmth of outdoor materials can turn a small urban terrace into a place of relaxation and tranquility.

The combination of materials and textures such as wood and decorative stones can transform a small terrace into a welcoming corner.

The use of aquatic elements in patios and gardens adds to a feeling of relaxation and tranquility. A small pool or fountain will create the perfect mood for enjoying the peace.

1 Using an awning or stretched canvas over the terrace can protect this outdoor space from the sun and enable it to be used any time of the day.

2 To protect privacy, you just have to use a fine lattice or position plants around the exterior perimeter.

3 Some types of outdoor furniture, such as certain benches, have an empty space inside, which makes them another option for storage.

4 If the furniture is exposed to the weather it must be made from weatherproof material like treated timber in order to guarantee its preservation.

5 In the warmer months, some terraces and patios can be used as a dining space, adding another room to the home.

6 Parterres or large plant pots decorate exterior spaces with no need to position lots of plants.

7 To optimize space, a good idea is to choose folding tables and chairs which can be put away to leave the space clear if necessary.

8 Hang window boxes from the railing to decorate narrow balconies.

9 Interior patios can be glassed in and decorated in a Japanese style, as a minimalist look is good in small spaces.

10 You can create a chill-out zone by adding a bench with simple cushions and small points of light.

ACKNOWLEDGEMENTS

Photographers:

Adrià Goula – p. 66, p. 90, p. 91, p. 109, p. 182 (below).
André Thoraval – p. 11, p. 40, p. 41.
Andrew Twort/Red Cover – p. 194 (below).
Beppe Giardino – p. 38, p. 82, p. 83, p. 120-121.
Caramel – p. 104.
Carlos Cezanne – p. 106, p. 107, p. 129, p. 130, p. 168, p. 169.
Carlos Domínguez – p. 30, p. 131, p. 170 (above), p. 171.
CJ Studio – p. 20 (above), p. 21, p. 139, p. 163.
Eugeni Pons – p. 14 (above), p. 174-175.
Frak Oudeman – p. 44, p. 48, p. 149.
Gary Chang – p. 19, p. 20 (below).
Gogortza & Llorella – p. 12, p. 13, p. 18, p. 39, p. 42, p. 43, p. 46, p. 54, p. 55, p. 64 (above), p. 65, p. 94, p. 95, p. 114, p. 115, p. 116, p. 117, p. 136, p. 142, p. 143, p. 154, p. 156, p. 160, p. 161.
Henry Wilson/Red Cover – p. 178, p. 179.
i29 – p. 78, p. 79, p. 80, p. 81, p. 138, p. 164 (above).
Ibarra Rosano Design Architects – p. 187.
James Wilkins – p. 70 (above), p. 112, p. 113.
Javier Haddad Conde – p. 76, p. 118, p. 119.
Joan Roig – p. 192.
John M. Hall – p. 14 (below), p. 15, p. 50, p. 51, p. 52 (above), p. 84, p. 85.
Jonathan Clark – p. 26, p. 27.
Jordi Jové/Arboretum – p. 181, p. 183, p. 184, p. 185, p. 188, p. 189, p. 190, p. 191, p. 196-197.
Jordi Miralles – p. 8-9, p. 32, p. 33, p. 47, p. 87 (above), p. 97, p. 158 (below), p. 162.
Luigi Filetici – p. 31 (above), p. 49, p. 57, p. 124.

Luuk Kramer – p. 45, p. 125, p. 137, p. 145.
Mattijs van Room – p. 92, p. 93, p.146, p. 176-177, p. 193.
Michael Moran – p. 186.
Mikiko Mikuyama – 25, p. 87 (below), p. 102 (above).
MoHen Design International/Maoder Chou – p. 24, p. 28, p. 29, p. 100, p. 101, p. 126, p. 141, p. 153, p. 155, p. 157.
Niall Cutton – p. 34, p. 35, p. 140, p. 158 (above), p. 172 (above).
Pablo Fernández Lorenzo – p. 98, p. 99, p. 110 (above), p. 164 (below), p. 165.
Paul Cha – p. 180.
Philip Vile – p. 16, p. 108, p. 122-123, p. 150, p. 172 (below).
Philip Tang – p. 86, p. 103, p. 110 (below), p. 111, p. 144.
Pino dell'Aquila, Walter Nicolino, Max Tomasinelli – p. 36, p. 37, p. 147.
Popeye Tsang – p. 68, p. 69, p. 74, p. 75.
Sandra Pereznieto – p. 10, p. 67, p. 88, p. 89, p. 127, p. 148.
Shania Shegedyn – p. 22, p. 23, p. 182 (above).
Sharrin Rees – p. 6 (right), p. 17, p. 56, p. 58, p. 59, p. 72, p. 73, p. 102 (below), p. 151.
Simon Devitt – p. 7 (left), p. 152.
Stephan Zähring – p. 52 (below), p. 53, p. 70 (below), p. 71, p. 96.
Teun van der Dries – p. 62-63.
Ulso Tsang – p. 6 (left), p. 60-61, p. 64 (below), p. 132, p. 133, p. 134, p. 135, p. 170 (below).
Undine Pröhl – p. 7 (right), p. 194 (right), p. 195.
Virgile Simon Betrand – p. 128, p. 166, p. 167.
ZECC Architecten, Cornbreadworks – p. 77.
Zooey Braun – p. 31 (below), p. 105, p. 159, p. 173.

Architects and interior designers:

Anthony Chan (www.chanarchitecture.com.au) – p. 128, p. 166, p. 167.

Arboretum (www.arboretum.es) – p. 181, p. 183, p. 184, p. 185, p. 188, p. 189, p. 190, p. 191, p. 196-197.

Arteks (www.arteksarquitectura.com) – p. 14 (above), p. 174-175.

AvroKO (www.avroko.com) – p. 46 (above), p. 114, p. 115.

Caramel (www.caramel.at) – p. 104.

Carlo Ratti Associati (www.carloratti.com) – p. 36, p. 37, p. 147.

CJ Studio – p. 20 (above), p. 21, p. 139, p. 163.

CSS Architecture (www.ccs-architecture.com) – p. 76, p. 118, p. 119.

Data AE (www.dataae.com) – p. 66, p. 90, p. 91, p. 109, p. 182 (below).

David Giovannitti – p. 186.

Dick van Gameren Architecten (www.dickvangameren.com) – p. 45, p. 125, p. 137, p. 145.

Double G – p. 11, p. 40, p. 41.

Dry Design (www.drydesign.com) – p. 7 (right), p. 194 (above), p. 195.

Faulkner & Chapman Landscape Design (www.faulknerchapman.com.au) – p. 182 (above).

Filippo Bombace (www.filippobombace.com) – p. 31 (above), p. 49, p. 57, p. 124.

Francesc Rifé (www.rife-design.com) – p. 12, p. 13, p. 54, p. 55, p. 154, p. 156, p. 160, p. 161.

Gary Chang, Jerry She/EDGE – p. 19, p. 20 (below).

Gary Chang, Raymond Chan/EDGE – p. 68, p. 69, p. 74, p. 75.

Hofman Dujardin Architecten (www.hofmandujardin.nl) – p. 92, p. 93, p. 146, p. 176-177, p. 193.

i29 (www.i29.nl) – p. 78, p. 79, p. 80, p. 81, p. 138, p. 164 (above).

Ibarra Rosano Design Architects (www.ibarrarosano.com) – p. 187.

Inés Rodríguez, Raúl Campderrich/Air projects (www.air-projects.com) – p. 87 (above).

Ippolito Fleitz Group (www.ifgroup.org) – p. 31 (below), p. 105, p. 159, p. 173.

Jabier Lekuona – p. 18, p. 39, p. 94, p. 95, p. 136.

Jaume Prior – p. 192.

Jonathan Clark Architects (www.jonathanclarkarchitects.co.uk) – p. 26, p. 27.

Jorge Queralt – p. 32, p. 33, p. 97.

Juan Antonio Gómez González/Cru (www.grupcru.com) – p. 42, p. 43, p. 46 (below), p. 64 (above), p. 65, p. 142.

Juan Luis Madariaga – p. 8-9, p. 158 (below), p. 162.

Judith Farran – p. 116, p. 117, p. 143.

Kim Utzon (www.utzon-arkitekter.dk) – p. 129, p. 130, p. 168, p. 169.

Lawrence Group (www.thelawrencegroup.com) – p. 48.

Leone Design Studio – p. 25, p. 87 (below), p. 102 (above).

Mackay and Partners (mackayandpartners.co.uk) – p. 34, p. 35, p. 140, p. 158 (above), p. 172 (above).

Ministry of Design (www.modonline.com) – p. 7 (left), p. 152.

Mohen Design International (www.mohen-design.com) – p. 24, p. 28, p. 29 p. 100, p. 101, p. 126, p. 141, p. 153, p. 155, p. 157.

nARCHITECTS (www.nARCHITECTS.com) – p. 44, p. 149.

New ID Interiors (www.new-id.co.uk) – p. 30, p. 131, p. 170 (above), p. 171.

Pablo Fernández Lorenzo, Pablo Redondo Díaz – p. 98, p. 99, p. 110 (above), p. 164 (below), p. 165.

Page Goolrick (www.goolrick.com) – p. 14 (below), p. 15, p. 50, p. 51, p. 52 (above), p. 84, p. 85.

Paul Cha (www.paulchaarchitect.com) – p. 180.

Paulo Cassio – p. 106, p. 107.

PTang Studio (www.ptangstudio.com) – p. 6 (left), p. 60-61, p. 64 (below), p. 86, p. 103, p. 110 (below), p. 111, p. 132, p. 133, p. 134, p. 135, p. 144, p. 170 (below).

Queeste Architecten (www.queestearchitecten.nl) – p. 62-63.

Rafael Berkowitz (www.rbarchitect.com) – p. 70 (above), p. 112, p. 113.

Rocío Fueyo – p. 47.

Smart Design Studio (www.smartdesignstudio.com) – p. 6 (right), p. 17, p. 56, p. 58, p. 59, p. 72, p. 73, p. 102 (below), p. 151.

StudioAta (www.studioata.com) – p. 38, p. 82, p. 83, p. 120-121.

Target Living (www.targetliving.com) – p. 16, p. 108, p. 122-123, p. 150, p. 172 (below).

Tom McCallum – p. 22, p. 23.

Xavi Serravinyals/Entre4parets – p. 10, p. 67, p. 88, p. 89, p. 127, p. 148.

YLAB/Yuste Laarmann Arquitectos, Jorge Rangel (stylist) – p. 52 (below), p. 53, p. 70 (below), p. 71, p. 96.

ZECC Architecten (www.zecc.nl) – p. 77.